Memories of Abuse, Life Lessons Learned and Victories Claimed!

KEEP YOUR PECKER IN YOUR PANTS

S. L. HUGHES

Keep Your Pecker In Your Pants
Memories of Abuse, Life Lessons Learned and Victories Claimed!

©2021 S. L. Hughes

ISBN: 978-1-09837-032-9

Request for information should be sent to
S.L.Hughes.Books@gmail.com

Acknowledgements

Throughout my journey of growth, reflection and introspection while writing this book, I have been blessed by the steadfast, loving support of an incredible group of beautiful beings, who supported and cared for me along my way.

Àjíké, Debby, Satira, for your insight, professional wisdom, and benevolent ears, urging me forward, thank you.

Erin A. Wiley, editor extraordinaire, throughout our process, you listened with both head and heart, allowing your suggestions, corrections and changes, to preserve my voice, clear, strong and authentic, bless you.

To Tiffany, the daughter of my heart, your strength inspires me.

To Venson, my true brother, ultimate seeker of the Divine, offering infinite love and fidelity.

To Michelle, your love lifts me, your music fills my soul and your modeling forgiveness, is God's grace in action.

Thank you all, for believing in my "possible."

To my heavenly angels, I think of you lovingly, often and call your names: Dan, David, Eugene Gert, Mildred, Natalie, Olivia, Philip and Robbie. May you continue your watch over me, whispering sweet melodies and loving words into my spirit, reminding me that you are always with me. You are not forgotten.

Dedicated to Those Who Know

This book is dedicated to those of us who have, hidden in our depths, remnants of the brave, broken children we once were. Those of us whose lives have been forever altered at the hands of insatiable sexual predators. Those of us who had our innocence shattered and dreams snatched from us, before they had even begun to form. We have survived, endured, even thrived, despite the soul crushing devastation of our trauma. Over time, layer by layer, we have navigated the process of exorcising the painful burdens of our past wounding. And with every layer unearthed and cut away, we are gradually healing and reclaiming the fullness of our entire being.

To those of you who have valiantly stood by and loved us in our brokenness, daring to reach in and touch the jagged, fragmented pieces of our hearts, minds and souls, seeking to support us in our quest to create a more vibrant life full of color, light and joy, we say, "thank you". Forgive us for the many times we pushed you away, unable to understand that your love allowed you to want to see past our pain, insecurities, and flawed definitions of love. In loving us, you sought only to help us unveil a more honest image of our true radiance, and we are grateful.

And to those beautiful beings who could no longer bear the seemingly insurmountable weight of each new dawn, but instead sought refuge and release in the taking of their own lives, I say, "fly with the angels," parading your luminous wings before a merciful God. It is neither my right nor my duty to judge or condemn your choice. Yet sadly, intertwined with the fragrant gossamer essence you leave behind, there remains an empty space, yearning to be filled, in the hearts of those who love you.

CONTENTS

ONE

BRAVE READER
My Gratitude, Thanks, and a Disclaimer or Two

Before you continue any further, allow me to state a few things. I do not consider myself a "writer", but simply a woman with things to say, experiences to share, and the hope that someone reading my words might find a bit of needed encouragement and reassurance in their continued efforts to press on. As a non-writer, I am asking in advance for your tolerance of my penchant for run-on, descriptive sentences. I simply cannot seem to help myself.

Also, and of the utmost importance, allow me to loudly proclaim that I am neither a therapist, nor a mental health care professional. Therefore, it is not my intention to presume to offer any psychological or mental health "advice" of any kind, as I am supremely not qualified. My thoughts and opinions are my own, based solely on my experiences and life lessons learned along the way.

I have written this book and shared my heart as part of my continuing quest to save myself, through the accounting and examination of various parts of my life's story. I seek to release myself from the emotional chains of my past, held firmly in place and expertly anchored by my long-held secrets; secrets that have been resolvedly and insidiously eroding the lining of my soul, throughout significant segments of my lifetime.

This is a memoir of sorts, comprised of my varied life occurrences and experiences, to the best of my honest recollection. There remain gaps in my memory, resulting from the emotional trauma, physical, and psychological abuse that I suffered at the hands of my abuser. There were also others who caused varied emotional harm along the way, even while professing their love for me, which you will read about later. Therefore, please do not feel the need to read this book in the order of chapter listing, as I am not recounting the events of my life in chronological order. You may instead wish to determine your reading order by looking at the chapter listing each time you open this book, then allowing yourself to be guided by your heart's wisdom and need of the moment.

Thankfully, over the years, with many hours and dollars invested in the expert guidance of several therapists, some of my memories have been recovered. Recovering various memories has helped me to breathe through the fog of pain that once defined what felt like my every waking moment. However, there are still memories that I cannot recover, which I am content, and perhaps a bit relieved, to leave tucked away in some distant pocket of my soul, for the time being. Perhaps these unrecovered memories are protecting me from a selection of emotional photographs that I am not yet ready to develop and explore. Or maybe these buried memories no longer have any relevant meaning to my present existence and therefore should not be excavated, but instead left where they are, in some long-forgotten pocket of my soul. Pockets, I've discovered, are a bit of a curious thing, in that they can be in equal parts useful and useless.

As you read, you will discover that I am writing in short biographical sections, offering an abbreviated narration of a particular event or time period in my life. I will sometimes then go on to share my self-discoveries gleaned from that specific situation. Lastly, I will offer a reflection, meditation, or mantra for your consideration. You will also find frequent opportunities for your own writing and reflection, in response to what I have put forward. Allow me to gently suggest that you also keep a writing journal nearby, as a loving companion, helping you to record whatever awakenings your soul may allow.

I am a woman of faith and will, with intention, draw on my faith as a source of inspiration and illustration for the reflections, meditations, and/or mantras that I pose. I do not ask or expect that you believe what I believe, or believe anything at all. However, it is my hope that you possess some type of a belief system and or faith in a "higher power", to help support and steady you, in your heart's exploration of this book.

Before beginning your personal, explorative journey in the reading of this book, I would propose that you give serious consideration to finding a licensed and qualified therapist, someone to assist you in your emotional grounding, soul exploration, and growth endeavors, connected to this book and beyond. Once you have found a therapist you feel you can work with, commit to the process! Do not be like me and waste time playing the game of what I call, "emotional peek-a-boo" with yourself and/or your therapist. In other words, do not try and hide your truth from yourself or your therapist. Be as honest as you can. Otherwise, why bother investing your time, energy, and money? It took me a long time to understand the importance of this, although I suspect that my current therapist would tell you that I sometimes do not practice what I preach.

If you already have a therapist whom you trust and have begun your "work", good for you. I encourage you to share this book with him or her, and then have a clear and honest discussion regarding whether this book is a potentially viable resource for you at this time in your journey and therapeutic process.

In this book, I hope that I have created a resource for both head and heart, something that I wish had been available for me when I began my journey of healing. Moving forward, should you find anything in what I share of my story that helps you and/or resonates with you in any way, I am glad and honor the insights that may arise within you. However, feel free to disregard any of what you read that does not resonate with your own soul's innate wisdom. I will not take offense. After all, I know only my own life's passages, with its twists and turns, ups and downs, ins and outs. I am still on my own soul's journey, as are you with yours. May we all travel safely, extending to ourselves merciful eyes and compassionate hearts.

Blessed Be...

A Moment of Reflection

As you are able, take a moment or two and reflect on the following.

Where are you in this present moment of your life's journey, as you continue your process and pursuit of healing in body, mind and spirit?

_____

_____

_____

_____

_____

_____

_____

_____

_____

_____

_____

_____

_____

_____

_____

_____

_____

_____

_____

_____

_____

_____

_____

What innate traits and/or developed qualities do you possess that have allowed you to survive to this very moment?

_____

_____

_____

_____

_____

_____

_____

_____

_____

_____

_____

_____

_____

_____

_____

_____

_____

_____

_____

_____

_____

What possible new and healthy skills and/or behaviors are you in the process of developing, that you believe will assist you in seeking continued wholeness, moving forward?

_____

_____

_____

_____

_____

_____

_____

_____

_____

_____

_____

_____

_____

_____

_____

_____

_____

_____

_____

_____

_____

_____

_____

A GENTLE AFFIRMATION OPPORTUNITY

Note: If you are unable and/or choose not to do this suggested affirmation process in this moment, wait and try another time, or not at all. Remember, you need not ever attempt any of what I propose. Listen to what your inner wisdom is telling you. Or you may want to try one of my meditative offerings in the presence and under the guidance of your therapist, or the two of you could possibly work together and create what works best for you.

Sit quietly, open your heart and repeat the following affirmations, if you are willing and/or able to do so. Speak them aloud or hold them softly in the stillness of your being, as guided by your soul's wisdom and heart's need. Move at your own pace. There is no right or wrong, there is only you, your breath, this moment.

I am still here.

There are wonderful gifts on my horizon, waiting for me to claim them.

I have everything within me that I need to grow and bloom.

I praise you Creator because I am fearfully and wonderfully made; your works are wonderful, this I know.   Psalm 139:14 NIV

I am marvelously made.

I rejoice in my being.

I welcome peace.

I open myself to light.

I open myself to love.

TWO: AN INTRODUCTION

Brave Reader,

Did you ever watch an episode of the original television series "Lost in Space", which aired between the years 1965 and 1968? The series was about the adventures of the Robinsons, a pioneering family of space colonists and their struggles to survive in outer space.

On their space journey, the Robinsons took a robot whose function was to not only provide technical information that was needed to aid the family in their space survival, but to also warn them of any possible dangers in the immediate area. When the Robot determined that danger was on the horizon, he could be counted on to siren out, "danger, danger (insert family/crew member name here), danger!"

Consider my written voice, in this moment, a gentle warning of possible "danger ahead" in this chapter. This will depend on where you find yourself in your healing journey of your experience of your abuse. If just reading the words, "possible danger ahead, use caution" causes you any level of anxiety, you may wish to stop, breathe and skip this chapter for now.

However, should you choose to read this chapter, you will see that I have written a letter to my abuser, whom I refer to as "my perpetrator". I call him "my" perpetrator, not out of any scintilla of affection or care, but rather as my way of acknowledging what was done to me, by him. I recognize that others may make use of another pronoun, which may feel less personal. My use of the word "my" reflects that, for me, there are few experiences more personal than sexual abuse and navigating the resulting trauma.

Please remember what I shared in Chapter One, regarding the order in which you read this book. For those of you who may not have read Chapter One, I offered the suggestion that you release yourself from the burden of reading and experiencing this book in chapter order, but instead allow yourself the freedom to follow the prompting and leading of your heart in selecting the chapter that you are most drawn to, when you open the book and peruse the table of contents.

Before reading this chapter, I again offer the gentle suggestion that if you are not in the head or heart space where you want to think about your abuser through the lens of writing a letter to him or her, you may want to give yourself permission to skip this section for now. If you have any trepidation whatsoever about whether you should read this, or any section in this book, I encourage you to stop and set it aside and come back to it at another time, if you so choose.

If all is well in your spirit and you choose to continue, then read on, fully empowered by the knowledge that you are always in charge of the choices you make regarding the way you allow yourself to explore and experience this book. Be kind to yourself in all things, especially those things contained in these pages. Honor the full weight of your truth.

Proceeding on…

TWO

KEEP YOUR PECKER IN YOUR PANTS, REV.
The Litany of "You", A Letter to My perpetrator

I am sixty-three years old now and how I wish that I could have written the following letter to my perpetrator, with its level of honesty and justified outrage, many years ago. However, I know now that there were things that I needed to learn before I could begin to discover and write my truth, as well as steps that I needed to take in order to reclaim my soul. I had to give myself time to identify the lies that I had been fed about who and what I was and then, with focused intent, regurgitate them out from the very depths of my being. I also needed to gain understanding of how to unapologetically and without shame or fear of reprisal, speak my own essential truth. But first, I had to open my entire being to the fact that my very existence mattered, that I had value, and that I matter, "just because."

The following words are some of the things that I wish I could have said to my perpetrator before he died. Would it have made any difference? Would I have been strong enough to say them? Probably not then, but I am strong enough now, so here goes.

Hello perpetrator (yes, the small "p" is intentional),

You are a lying, sanctimonious, two-faced, joy-stealing, monster.

You do unspeakable things to innocent, defenseless children, exercising your demonic power over their lives, secure in your ability to bend small bodies and pure souls, to your twisted will, ultimately robbing fragile hearts of their wide-eyed sense of wonder.

May God have mercy on you.

You deposit spores of rotten seeds in the wake of your ravaging plunder, deep in the psyche of your victims. Seeds that will sadly, one day birth a myriad of undeserved feelings of ugliness, shame, fear, crippling depression, heartache, sometimes unbearable emotional and psychological pain, self-loathing, angst, and the ever-present siren's call of suicide, imprinted on the fragile souls of your victims. In short, perpetrator, you are a bastard.

May God have mercy on you.

You identify, stalk, groom, and capture your defenseless prey, treating them as though they were a side dish on the banquet table of your twisted feast, acting as though these precious, blameless innocents have been presented for your gluttonous, depraved pleasure and wicked appetite, arrayed for your insultingly casual perusal and ultimate consumption, like the sweetest and rarest of forbidden delicacies.

May God have mercy on you.

With audacious disrespect, you put on your clerical collar, cloak your rotting soul-less carcass in your self-proclaimed holy robes, resplendent in rich colors of reds, purples, dark luxurious ebony, trimmed in the richest of gold and silver shimmering threads. Then you dare to add the final insulting touch to all that is sacred and adorn yourself in the most precious of all jewels, the cross of Christ. Your lying tongue then espouses your service, love and devotion to the Creator. You disgust me.

May God have mercy on you.

You stand in your pulpit, hiding behind your pagan altar, spouting Bible verses, picking and choosing passages that suit you, king of your self-created kingdom, declaring that God has "called" you to minister to those in need of spiritual direction and guidance. You repulse me.

May God have mercy on you.

Do you sleep peacefully at night or are you afraid to close your eyes, lest you hear the cries, whimpers and pleadings of those you have harmed almost beyond measure, beckoning to you in your dreams? I hope that you are tormented nightly by the weight of your sins, although I am doubtful that you possess any whisper of conscience which would permit you to be so.

May God have mercy on you.

You are a vile misfeasor, and you should be afraid of the very God whose name you so casually call upon during your theatrical performances, that you seek to pass off as worship. The very sight of you sickens me, as you peer down your haughty nose at those you deem without the power or internal godliness needed to achieve your level of self-knighted sanctity.

May God have mercy on you.

You fill my mouth with bile as you calmly reach out your unclean and guilty hands to bless, anoint, and pray over the trusting and unsuspecting. You, who should be shepherd but are in truth wolf, as you with cunning and lustful greed, look into the eyes of your unwary flock, deciding who you will devour next. You should fear the God you so deceitfully claim to know.

May God have mercy on you and your unsuspecting flock.

You have made a lifetime of hiding your base nature in plain sight of those who respect, even revere you, blind to your evil truth. I was like them once, blind to and afraid of the ravenous demon in you. I, however, am no longer blind to, or afraid of your wickedness. I "see" you and you no longer have any power over me. I am no longer the frightened, defenseless child you manipulated, took advantage of and almost destroyed. I am strong.

And you, Rev., can go straight to hell but in the meantime, "keep your damn pecker in your pants!"

A Check in of Head and Heart

How are you feeling? Do you feel stressed, anxious or triggered in any way, by what you have just read? Has your breathing pattern changed, is your chest tight, or do you have any pain or tightness in any part of your body? Are you feeling teary, do you have the beginnings of a headache, and/or are you feeling in any way "out of sorts"?

If you answered "yes" to any of the questions I just asked, perhaps now would be a good time for you to stop, take a break, do some deep breathing, or even close this book for a while. Or would you like to try some writing to help clear your spirit of any thoughts and/or feelings that have arisen?

_____

_____

_____

_____

_____

_____

_____

_____

_____

_____

_____

_____

_____

_____

_____

_____

_____

_____

_____

_____

_____

_____

_____

_____

_____

_____

_____

_____

_____

_____

_____

_____

_____

_____

_____

_____

_____

Please make sure that you feel ready to continue with the following empowering reading and reflection. If not, there's always another time, or not at all. You get to decide.

Meditation and Reflection Opportunity

Perhaps, there are things that you have wanted to say to your perpetrator for a long time and were not in a place and space in your heart or head to safely do so. Maybe today, you can begin your process of healthy venting and emotional purging, by writing down your thoughts and feelings about your perpetrator, even if it is only one word on a page at a time.

Kicking and screaming all the way, I have discovered that writing can be an empowering and liberating exercise and opportunity, creating an emotional sanctuary, a readily accessible haven to release oneself from potentially harmful thoughts and feelings. Thoughts and feelings that have possibly resulted from hurts so deep, that there are sometimes no spoken words to describe them.

Is there a letter that you need to write to yourself or someone else? If so, treat yourself to a brand-new journal and get started. Or reacquaint yourself with one of your old journals that you have cast aside. Get creative in your selection or you may even enjoy making one of your own.

Be aware that, if you are writing a letter to someone else, you do not have to mail it. It is the act of writing that is for your benefit. What you do with your letter is a discussion for you, your therapist, your common sense and your heart, to decide.

Always remember that I am in no way attempting to advise you on navigating the ever-changing seas of your life. Rather, I am sharing with you some of what I have learned and how I am healing my own fragile, yet oddly and wonderfully resilient heart.

THREE

SWALLOWING TEARS AND TWIZZLERS

I have courted and maintained a love-hate relationship with food for what has felt like my entire life. This relationship began when, as a child, I needed a way to ease and comfort my aching heart and to stop the seemingly endless, ocean's flow of my tears.

Looking back, I can remember crying in my bedroom alone and afraid, day after day, night after night, as I waited for "him" to come down the hall, stand outside my door and jiggle the knob in the hope that I had forgotten to lock it. I would lie in my bed, curled in a tight ball, trying to make myself as small as possible and cry hot anguished tears, while praying fervently that "maybe this time," he would just give up and go away. As I huddled shaking in my bed, I yearned desperately for someone to come and save me. No one came. I was ten.

My days marched on relentlessly of their own accord, blurring with pain and confusion, one into another, resulting in me becoming more unhappy, fearful and watchful. Each passing day, bit by bit, losing my childhood joy and innocence. I was either crying all the time or fighting desperately not to cry all the time because, as I came to learn, there was no room or safe space for my tears in the carefully constructed façade that was my life.

Evidence of my tears raised too many questions that the adults in my life did not appear to want to know the answers to. They wanted me smiling, happy, and singing God's praises like the "good little girl" they were raising me to be. To them, I had everything a little girl could possibly want: a beautiful house to live in, food to eat, a mother, stepfather, grandparents, aunts, uncles and assorted other relatives who loved and adored me. What could I possibly have to cry about?

And so, I did as I was told and attended Sunday school, church, sang in the children's choir, got good grades in school, and did my chores, smiling all the while. I knew the role that I was supposed to play in my life's drama, and I set out to play it perfectly, like a never-ending game of "pretend". I thought that maybe, if I excelled in the portrayal of a "good little girl", maybe then the adults in my life would finally step into their assigned roles and love me enough to make the pain stop and release me from the hell that I was living in. However, in order to perfect my role, I had to stop my tears and if I could not stop them, I needed to learn to hide them because clearly and in acting terminology, there were no tears written for my character's profile or motivation.

Hiding my tears was easier said than done. My heart was breaking, and I was slowly unraveling inside my soul. I felt unloved, unprotected, defenseless, always afraid and alone with my secret shame of what "he" was doing to me. It would be years before I would come to understand that this sense of shame that I carried was not mine to call my own.

Over time, I discovered that when I was eating, I had something else to focus on. Something that not only tasted good, but that somehow also felt good and I could stop crying for periods of time and somehow function in a way that was considered "normal." I thought, "problem solved, no more tears," as I now had a plan of action. When I wanted to cry, I could eat instead. When "he" hurt me, I could eat more. And when I felt alone and afraid, I could eat even more. Soon I was a whirlwind of tears and: Tasty-cakes, Reese's Peanut Butter Cups, Utz Potato Chips, Baby Ruth bars, Sugar Babies, Junior

Mints, Milky Ways, Three Musketeer Bars and one of my all-time favorites, Twizzlers, to name a few. Almost no candy or cake was off limits to me, in my efforts to stem the increasing tide of my tears.

Looking back, I think I thought that if I could somehow stop my tears, I could distance myself from the pain of waking up to face yet another day. But the brightness of each new dawn insistently greeted me and lingered, like an uninvited guest, tethering me to my heartache, which always threatened to burst free and consume me.

Eventually, I would come to learn that tears have a mind of their own and that they do not just go away. My tears were still inside of me, waiting and planning creative ways to get my attention, as they were smothered under what was becoming pounds and pounds of food. At the time, I was too young and emotionally unequipped to understand that my tears were like having my very own built in warning system, trying their best to alert me that something was very wrong inside my soul. And I, not understanding their message, sought to silence them with food.

Little did I know that in silencing my tears, I would be preventing myself from developing some of the very coping skills and strengths that I would need to endure the stormy days that lay ahead. My tears were trying desperately to get my attention and help me save myself from destruction. But I ran from them and added new foods to my arsenal of the tools and tricks that were designed to help me continue my pretense of normalcy.

Some days, I would swear I could practically hear the cupcakes calling and cooing encouraging and loving words to me with every bite, words and phrases such as, "everything will be OK," or my twisty Twizzlers saying, "be strong, we'll get through this together." Food was my faithful friend, confidant, protector, even a savior of sorts, always there waiting patiently for my return. I had finally found something to fill up the hole in my heart and yet, I was never satisfied or filled.

It would be many years and therapy dollars later before I would come to understand that food was not my friend and that I had developed a codependent relationship of sorts with food, and it was killing me. The very food that I had used as a child to smother my tears, was now smothering me as an adult.

Gentle and Loving Introspection Opportunity

Has there been a need for you to quiet and/or hide your tears at times? How have you managed to do this?

_____

_____

_____

_____

_____

_____

_____

_____

_____

_____

_____

_____

_____

_____

_____

_____

_____

_____

_____

_____

_____

_____

_____

Repeat the following phrases, as you choose and/or are able. Allow time for a few cleansing breaths after each phrase.

I honor my tears and I thank them for doing their job.

I am grateful for the potential insights and awareness that my tears may offer.

Crying does not make me weak.

I give myself the gift of my tears when they are needed.

There is joy in the morning light.

Is it time to write some of what is on your heart?

_____

_____

_____

_____

_____

_____

_____

_____

_____

_____

_____

_____

_____

_____

IT IS GOOD TO SOOTHE THE SOUL

Are you in need of a gentle, warm hug, in body, mind or spirit? If so, perhaps now might be a good time to stop, and oh so gently, allow your arms to wrap around yourself as you are able. If you cannot accomplish this physically, allow your hug to enfold you in your mind and spirit.

Feel the warmth of your own loving and nurturing thoughts surrounding you, soothing you and holding you. As you need, experiment with allowing your body to sway or rock in a rhythm that is unique only to you and what you require in this moment.

Remember to breathe. Know that you are safe. Send love and light into those areas of your being, patiently waiting to receive.

FOUR

NO!

Today, I unexpectedly found myself saying "yes" to something that someone else wanted me to do, although it was not anything that I wanted to
do at all. This ultimately created a great deal of anxiety and frustration inside
of me. Saying "yes" in this instance led me to stop and reflect on numerous
other times in my life when I had been far too quick with my "yes", instead
of stating an unequivocable and unapologetic "no."

In truth, there have been many times in my life when I have spoken a
somewhat tepid "yes" to someone else's request, while secretly yearning to
respond with a bold, declarative "no, hell no, F-U no, kiss my whole entire
ass no, get out of my face with that nonsense no," or better yet, a simple,
elegant yet powerful "no", that would literally stop people in their tracks. I
have, at times, even joyfully envisioned that when confronted with someone
else's need of my "yes", I would instead say "no", then turn and sashay (what
a great word!) away, feeling strong and in control, shutting the door to any
possible discussion or debate, leaving no room for angst or anxiety to make
a home in my spirit.

However, today I again heard myself uttering a resigned and wimpy
"yes", as though I had no will or authority of my own to herald my "no". I
felt as though I had failed myself by doing what appeared, on the surface,
to be the easy, nonconfrontational thing to do. Sadly, I gave in to someone

else's needs and wants without thought or care for my own, and by doing so, risked and abandoned my own power and peace of mind.

"No" is such a small little word, comprised of only two letters, perhaps causing some to believe that the use of it would present no challenge at all. But I say, "Au contraire, Mon Cheri". "No" is not a small insignificant word at all, but rather a big fat loud, bold word, hiding behind two skinny letters, secretly possessing the potential for a great deal of voluminous power.

I have learned over the years that understanding, claiming, and implementing the sustained usage of the powerful little "no" can at times be a difficult task for incest survivors like myself to accomplish. I have spoken to other survivors who have expressed variations of the same sentiment, regarding their repeated and frustrating inability to invoke the power of "no" and use it for their personal well-being.

It has been challenging, at times, to explain this difficulty to those who have not been an incest victim themselves, suffered any type of physical, mental or emotional abuse, or supported an abuse victim through their journey of healing. To attempt an explanation of what it means and how it feels to lose one's power and control over their personhood, because of their inability to say "no", can be quite frustrating. This needed power and survival trait was callously stolen from those of us who are survivors, by our abusers and often others as well.

As a child, my power of "no" was weeded out of me, systematically it seemed, by the elders responsible for my care. They instructed me (I imagine with the best of intentions) in what it meant to be a "good little girl", telling me that being a "good little girl" was something that I should aspire to be at all times. They repeated time and again that one of the main characteristics found in a "good little girl", other than loving Jesus wholeheartedly, was the desire and ability to always obey Jesus and my elders. This meant that I was never to question an elder about anything they asked me to do, nor could I be so boldly disrespectful as to refuse to obey a command or directive given to me by an elder.

I was indoctrinated into the belief that, if an adult instructed me to do something, my only answer should be "yes ma'am" or "yes sir", without question or hesitation. The thought of saying "no, I don't want to", "I'm not going to", or "I can't" was never even a remote consideration on my part, lest I be regarded by an elder as being disrespectful or having a "smart mouth", neither of which would be tolerated under any circumstances, in my household.

Growing up, the punishment for being disrespectful to an elder would be swift and severe and ranged from a simple "talking to" (meaning a dressing down), or several licks on the legs or behind with a switch from the tree in our back yard. But the rewards for being obedient and submissive were great and could be as enticing as special sweet treats, new clothes, shoes or even a new toy when it wasn't even a birthday or Christmas! As a result of these incentives, I sought to behave in ways as to not be punished and I almost never was. I answered, "yes ma'am" and "yes sir" to almost everything requested of me by my elders, at almost all times.

The system of child raising used on me by my elders was one that reflected the mindset of "yes" equals obedience, and obedience equals good, and good equals reward. At the same time, it showed that "no" equals bad, which equals unacceptable, which equals punishment and worse, meant unlovable. It was flawed and it was dysfunctional. Perhaps it was all that the elders themselves knew to do. Nevertheless, this deeply broken and destructive way of child rearing, held firmly in place by generations of elders before I was even born, each generation passing it down to the next, paved the way for my brokenness and heartache to come.

The "yes equals good, no equals bad" child raising model left a deep imprint on my soul, and I would eventually come to see how easy it was for my perpetrator to manipulate, intimidate and control me. He held all the power of both the "no" and the "yes", while I, as a child, held none. I was too young to understand that there was a power dynamic on the table and that I was in no position to claim it.

Unfortunately, my learned childhood inability to say "no", and fear of being found unworthy of love, would become a life-long pattern, awakening harmful and self-destructive aspects of my personality and temperament. It would cause me to endure and attempt to manage bouts of depression, thoughts of self-harm, repressed emotions, resentment and a parade of unhealthy relationships in and out of my life.

After a good deal of therapy and prayerful self-compassion, I have learned of the soul-keeping and liberating use of my "no". I realize that I must practice daily vigilance in monitoring and listening carefully to my heart's desires. I have to check in with my self-preservation instincts and good common sense, before I respond to others with a careless "yes", instead of a healthy, sanity preserving "no", lest I slip back into my old peacekeeping, just do what seems easy in the moment ways. Perhaps I should embrace the wisdom of those who have said, "no is a complete sentence!"

Today, I rejoice and celebrate my power of "no" and I have no intention of ever giving it up! There is no need for me to be a "good little girl" any longer!

A Realization and Reflection

I have come to realize that my use of words and phrases like "maybe", "perhaps", and "let me think about it" have often been stalling tactics that I have used for the times that I have really wanted to say "no" but lacked the courage and conviction to do so. My goal is to eliminate as many unnecessary "maybes and perhaps-es and let me think about its" as possible, from my linguistic profile.

Gently Ask Yourself…

Are there words or phrases that I sometimes use as stalling tactics when I am hesitant or at times even afraid to say, "no"?

_____

_____

_____

_____

_____

_____

_____

_____

_____

_____

_____

_____

_____

_____

_____

What words or phrases can I discover, claim and use, to help me more fully embrace my power of "no?"

_____

_____

_____

_____

_____

_____

_____

_____

_____

_____

_____

_____

_____

_____

_____

_____

_____

_____

_____

_____

_____

What effect does saying "yes", when I want to say "no", sometimes have on me in body, mind and/or spirit?

_____

_____

_____

_____

_____

_____

_____

_____

_____

_____

_____

_____

_____

_____

_____

_____

_____

_____

_____

Realization and Meditation Moment

Discovering my power of "no" has given my head, heart, and spirit the gift of more fully appreciating the power of my "yes". I have found that when I do not have large portions of my emotional, mental and physical energy drained by having to process and at times fight for my power of "no", I am free to answer a joyful and fully empowered "yes" to those things which feed, uplift and liberate my soul.

My "yes" moments have helped to create deeply meaningful opportunities of insight, growth and peace within my spirit, allowing me to discover more of who Spirit is calling me to be.

Consider taking a moment or two to reflect and then write about one of your most cherished "yes" experiences.

_____

_____

_____

_____

_____

_____

_____

_____

_____

_____

_____

_____

_____

Would it be helpful to ask yourself, "how can I create more joyous, healthy "yes" opportunities in my life?"

_____

_____

_____

_____

_____

_____

_____

_____

_____

_____

_____

_____

_____

_____

_____

_____

_____

_____

_____

_____

_____

_____

_____

A Final "yes, no" Thought

I have found that my "yes" and/or "no" answers do not always have to be monumental, life altering occurrences that turn my entire world upside down. They can be small, easy responses that, with practice, create a pattern of giving myself permission to respond in intuitive and emotionally healthy ways that answer and fulfill my own heart's desires.

When I embrace my "yes" or "no" power from a place of truth and honor of self, I am more likely to make decisions about my life that are practical, healing and soul fulfilling. This keeps me aligned with my desire to move through the world in a way that I neither knowingly or willingly cause harm to myself or others.

Do you have any final "yes/no" thoughts, reflections and or insights?

_____

_____

_____

_____

_____

_____

_____

_____

_____

_____

_____

_____

_____

A MOMENT OF SOUL NOURISHING

Let's take a break from reading and reflecting and engage in a little soul nourishing…

Make a list of ways in which you can nourish yourself in body, mind, and/or spirit. Once you have started your list, keep it easily accessible and add to it as new thoughts and ideas arise. You may even want to make copies and place them in various places, so that this list serves as a reminder to take care of yourself from the inside out.

Get creative as you add to your "soul nourishing list", keeping in mind that not everything has to have a cost attached to it. Add things that are large and small. You are worthy and deserving of good things!

Here is something that I have on my list in several different places, because otherwise I have the tendency to forget. Having it written down holds me to a needed and loving level of self-accountability.

"Today, I will set aside time of quiet to spend with myself, breathing in peace."

Feel free to add other words or phrases that are meaningful to you.

Ways in Which I Can Nourish My Soul

After completing your list and when you are ready to proceed, read on, extending yourself the gifts of patience, acceptance and love.

_____

_____

_____

_____

_____

_____

_____

_____

_____

_____

_____

_____

_____

_____

_____

_____

_____

_____

_____

_____

FIVE

THERE ARE MONSTERS
IN MY DREAMS, GRANDMA

I stand in the narrow, unlit hallway, hurting, trembling and confused, with fat, hot tears running down my face, looking over my shoulder, praying that my perpetrator is not nearby, listening, ready to yank the phone out of my hand, as with shaking fingers, I hit the buttons on the touchtone phone and call my grandmother. When she answers, in halting whispers with breathing made ragged by the heavy flow of my tears, I tell her about him and what he has just done to me.

Using words that no child should ever have to utter, I tell my grandmother the awful truth of how he grabbed me by my wrist, pulled me to him, and forced his mouth on mine. I tell her of the awful feeling of helplessness, of the foul taste of him, I tell her everything. I tell her because I know that she loves me and that she will come and save me from him. I tell her that he is ugly like a monster, as he touches me in my secret, sacred places.

As I pour out my heavy, fractured heart to my grandmother, I know for certain that she will come and save me from him. In my mind and heart, my grandmother is like a superhero and her love for me is her ultimate superpower. And with my child-like faith and trust in her, I believe that she will come and free me from the hell that has become my life.

I beg my grandmother to come and take me home with her. I want her to take me back to the home I love, where she and I can once again bake cakes and sing songs and laugh and hang clothes on the clothesline in the backyard, while breathing in their clean freshness. I yearn to go home with my grandmother, where there are endless days of bright sun and no secret shadows filling the corners. Home with her, where I can move freely from room to room without fear of something evil lurking, waiting to grab me and devour me, bit by bit. I know for certain that my beloved grandma will come save me because she loves me. Grandma loves me more than anything or anyone in the whole world and she has told me this every day of my life. I know that she will surely come for me.

My grandmother listened quietly to me, as I spoke to her of the secret, unspeakable horrors of my days. When I was finished talking, there was a heavy silence, and then she gently said, "it was just a bad dream baby, nothing more, nothing happened, go back to sleep and remember that grandma loves you so much and I will see you on the weekend. And I will bake you your favorite cake as a special treat, and you can play with your baby dolls." She went on to say, "don't tell anyone what you told me because it did not really happen, remember, it was just a dream, a bad dream with a monster in it, just a dream". It was 3:30 in the afternoon, I had not been sleeping and I had not been dreaming.

As I listened to my grandmother trying to convince me of bad dreams with monsters in them, I stood stunned, my tiny world collapsing, all hope of being rescued, gone. My superhero grandmother, who had always told me how very precious I was to her and how much she loved me, was not coming to save me. I was alone with the monster.

I do not remember the end of my conversation with my grandmother, nor do I remember even hanging up the phone. I have no memory of anything after that day and for many days, perhaps weeks afterwards. It was as though an entire block of time simply disappeared from my mind.

This sense of missing blocks of time would happen to me repeatedly in the years to come. Looking back, I think of these episodes of having chunks of time disappear from my memory, as periodic chasms that would open in my heart and swallow my pain, temporarily removing the worst of my encounters with the monster, so that I could still function. The chasm would then close, sealing my heartache deep into its fathomless depths, allowing my life to go on, to limp on.

Although I do not recall anything that happened after I spoke to my grandmother that fateful day, I do remember the painful and life-changing lessons that I learned. I learned that my grandmother was not a superhero. I learned that regardless of what she had always told me, grandma did not love me enough to come and save me. I learned that love hurts and often disappoints. I learned that love could not be trusted, and that I was left alone to deal with the monster that lived in my dreams. I also learned that I could not always trust myself with what I thought was true. Perhaps it was indeed all a bad dream, as my grandmother had said.

My grandmother and I never spoke of that day, nor of dreams and monsters. I never told her that what she said to me on that day fractured my soul almost beyond repair. That it wounded me in a way that would leave me emotionally scarred and crippled for years to come, leaving bleeding cancerous wounds on my soul, so horrific, that I could not bear to touch them. Some days, I could not bear to look at myself in the mirror, for fear that I would see myself covered in the emotional equivalent of gangrenous, pus-filled ulcers.

After that day, I knew that the monster's power was stronger than even my beloved grandmother's love and ability to save me. I was beyond and perhaps unworthy of saving. The monster in my dreams was now loose in my life, during the day. He had won. His power was stronger than anyone I knew. No one was coming to help me and no one could save me. I was ten.

Reflection: The Monsters Are Not in Charge!

Thank God for Jesus and therapy! It would be many years before I would learn new truths to replace the old lies and lessons learned during my pain and heartache, that periodically held me bound in places of sadness, despair, desperation and hopelessness. I had to learn new truths about myself and others as well.

I have learned:

There are no real monsters, but there are real people who choose to do monstrous things.

I am stronger and more powerful than any monster that seeks to harm me.

I can "save" myself, and if it ever feels as though I cannot "save" myself, I can, should and will ask for help.

The best way to rid myself of monsters and nightmares is to turn on the light, because monsters fear the light.

I am worth saving!

I can be my own Superhero! I am my own Super-Shero!

My grandmother was not a superhero. She did not have a magic cape to put on and fly to my rescue on that awful day that I called her. My grandmother loved me in the only way she knew how. I forgive her for not being who I needed her to be, when I needed her most. She was, after all, only human.

A Question for Your Amazing Heart:

Sometimes, just getting out of bed in the morning makes someone a super-hero! In what way or ways, are you your own superhero?

_____

_____

_____

_____

_____

_____

_____

_____

_____

_____

_____

_____

_____

_____

_____

_____

_____

_____

_____

_____

_____

_____

A BREAK FROM WRITING

Would you like to take a break from writing? How about try drawing some of what is on your heart? Use whatever materials you have available, pen, pencil, crayons or more. Feel free to draw in this book, your journal or someplace else that feels right for to you.

Let your heart open and your imagination soar and just draw, even if it's just squiggles and dots on a page, they're your squiggles and dots, so they matter, a lot!

SIX

LOVES ME, LOVES ME NOT!

After he tore from me what was not his to have, he almost always told me that he loved me.

Nothing that he did to me was about love.

He would often press money into my hands, as though he was presenting me with a gift, telling me to buy myself "something nice". If I refused, he would then demand that I take his dirty money. And he would whisper to me in his low-throated insidious way, making me want to take a bath to rid myself of his stench: "Don't tell your mother."

He offered me money, treating me like I was a whore whose body he had bought and paid for.

This was not love.

I would spend years of my life trying to unravel the twisted, demented model of what he called love. I would wander down self-destructive paths, searching for a love that would not hurt or make me feel bad, only to end up time after time, tired, angry, resentful, unhappy, afraid, feeling alone and unloved within myself and within the relationship of the moment.

I had no love to give and was unable to receive love, convinced that I was undeserving.

Thankfully, with the passing of time, good therapy, prayer, and a supportive friend or two, I came to understand and create my own definition of what love could and should look, feel, smell, taste and sound like, for me.

It would take a bit longer before I could allow myself to experience the full joy of love, but I did. I had been taught what love was not and now, I set out to learn all that love can be.

The Way of Love: *1 Corinthians 13: 4-7, The Message*

Love never gives up.

Love cares more for others than for self.

Love doesn't want what it doesn't have.

Love doesn't strut,

Doesn't have a swelled head,

Doesn't force itself on others,

Isn't always "me, first,"

Doesn't fly off the handle,

Doesn't keep score of the sins of others,

Doesn't revel when others grovel,

Takes pleasure in the flowering of truth,

Puts up with anything,

Trusts God always,

Always looks for the best,

Never looks back,

But keeps going to the end

Reflecting on Love

No matter how many times I read, recite, or hear this Scripture passage, I never fail to be moved by the simple, yet profound declarations of what love is or is not. These words have served as a reminder to me over the years of all that love can be, when one earnestly seeks to give and receive it in its purest form. I have used this passage as a basis for what I call my:

Love List

Love does not give up easily but is willing to go the distance.

Love cares for the needs and well-being of others in ways that allow for mutual respect, nurturing and growth.

Love does not want or not seek to possess what it does not have a right to claim as its own.

Love does not strut, does not have a swelled head and does not make empty gestures in front of others to be thought of in favorable terms, while in private, offering nothing.

Does not force itself on others, period.

Is not always shouting "me, first" but rather embraces the ideal of "give and take" challenging itself to understand and live out the process.

Does not fly off the handle but strives for patience and understanding.

Is a tireless communicator, willing to learn another's language, verbal and nonverbal.

Love fights fair for the good and health of the relationship.

Does not keep score of the wrongs of others, while absolving itself of any faults or failures.

Does not rejoice in causing another's pain or discomfort.

Does not revel when others grovel and has no need to make another feel inferior, to feel good about itself.

Takes pleasure in the flowering of truth, and seeks to plant seeds of care, kindness, compassion and sincerity, to create fertile ground for truth to grow and bloom.

Is willing to be inconvenienced, flexible and seeks to compromise, asking only that these efforts be returned in some measure or portion.

Always looks for the best and does not immediately anticipate the worst.

Never looks back, or revisits hurts once they have been resolved in a way that is mutually satisfactory and agreed upon.

Love seeks honesty and fairness.

Love keeps an open heart.

Love believes in its power to bring about change for the good of all.

Love trusts God always.

Love has no beginning or end.

Love looks like the smile in a baby's eyes, feels like the velvety petal of a rose, smells like a beautiful summer day after a rain shower when the air is clean and fresh, and tastes like endless possibilities, guided by hope and fueled by God's light.

Love sounds like music in the soul.

Love is all these things and more.

Now that you have read my Love List, perhaps you might like to make one of your own. Let your love list, serve as a reminder of what you want and need healthy love to look, feel, smell, taste and sound like, for you. Allow love to come alive in your spirit and reveal itself in all its splendor!

My Love List

A LOVE LETTER TO SELF

When was the last time you stopped to reflect on just how wonderful you really are? Do you realize that you are an amazing being with limitless potential, capable of doing incredible things? Do you understand that you possess within your depths, an abundance of gifts and talents that are unique only to you?

This moment offers an excellent opportunity for you to write yourself a love letter. What loving words and affirmations can you offer yourself in this moment? What are the words your soul longs to hear?

Release yourself from the need to be perfect. Only God's love is perfect. We mortal beings are gloriously and imperfectly flawed, yet oh so worthy of receiving and giving love to self and others.

Go ahead and begin your letter. You can do it. You may find it easier to write than you originally thought and more needed than you know. Seriously, begin. Your heart is waiting.

_____

_____

_____

_____

_____

_____

_____

SEVEN

JUST JESUS AND ME

I lay in the bed with my eyes squeezed tightly shut, my legs forced wide, as Sunday School melodies once again danced in my mind as the perpetrator hurt me. *"Jesus loves me, this I know, for the Bible tells me so."* I could hear the words ringing in my head, as though stuck on an endless loop, like a scratchy old album playing on an antiquated record player. With child-like faith I clung to the melodious promises of a kind and loving Savior who could, and would, make everything alright for me.

As I lay there, waiting for him to be done with me, I tell myself, "God will save me." But there was no mighty God or gentle Savior in the torturous bed with me. There was only me, him and what turned out to be meaningless hymns, laden with empty promises, playing round and round inside my head, mocking and daring me to continue my belief in the intervention of a "divine Savior".

"Love lifted me, love lifted me,
when nothing else could help, love lifted me."

In Sunday School, we learned that if we were bad and sinned, God would punish us and send us to hell to be with the devil for all eternity. But I was already in hell. Did this mean that I had sinned? Was I so bad that God felt the need to punish me here on Earth, as opposed to sending me directly to hell? How many sins could I have possibly committed by the age of ten, that would require the kind of punishment the perpetrator doled out to me whenever it suited him? Did Jesus not love me anymore, or had Jesus simply taken the equivalent of a coffee break while I was being ravaged by the devil himself? All I had were my questions, with no answers in sight.

"Jesus loves the little children, red and yellow, black and white, they are precious in His sight!"

On Sunday mornings, I sang with religious fervor of a loving, protective, compassionate, kind and forgiving Savior. But after church ended, I knew the unspoken truth of another so-called Savior and God. I knew of a God who was distant, cold and apathetic. I knew of a Jesus who, regardless of what the hymns promised, had no time nor care for my life.

"Blessed assurance, Jesus is mine."

How was it possible that I could feel the love of Jesus surrounding me on Sundays, but by mid-week, I could not feel the Savior's loving presence near me at all? This dichotomy between what I thought of as the loving Jesus I sang about on Sunday, and the One who deserted me the rest of the week, was the beginning of what I thought of as my "on again, off again, love-hate relationship" with God, Jesus and Spirit. I would worship, praise and exult the name of God with one breath, and then with another breath, denounce this same God as being an empty myth, offering me nothing.

"I must tell Jesus, all of my troubles, I cannot bear these burdens alone."

My "love-hate" relationship with the Divine resulted in me experiencing long periods in my life when I could not sing, pray or even speak the name of Jesus because my anger with Him was such a pulsating force in my mind and heart. My anger with Jesus occupied nearly all of my "praise space", blocking my direct access to Him. I shut my heart's door to God, while secretly longing, even daring Him to open it, enter and reveal Himself in all

His glorious power that I used to sing about. I needed God to finally claim me as His own and prove that He had not abandoned me, so that I could trust Him with my whole heart.

"I need thee O I need thee, every hour I need thee."

The years flew by, and I continued my love-hate tango with the Almighty. I was growing weary of the dance and tired of pretending that I was in relationship with the God I sang about on Sunday mornings, as I played the piano, sang or directed the choir. Jesus was not showing up for me and I was running out of patience with Him.

"I once was lost but now am found, was blind but now I see."

One day, for no apparent reason that I could fathom, something shifted in my spirit and I unexpectedly found myself wanting to try again with Jesus. It was almost like going back to an old flame, with whom I had once found a great and exceptional love like no other. I needed to believe that things between Jesus and I would be better this time and that there would be no empty promises. I gently, and with trepidation, opened my heart's door.

There was no movie-like epiphany moment of white light, singing angels, parting heavens and God appearing to me in a cloud, that would eventually lead me back to Jesus. But as I began reflecting on various twists and turns of my life, I began to recognize that God had repeatedly extended love and mercy for me in ways that I did not have eyes or heart to see.

"O how I love Jesus because He first loved me."

I was tired of being angry with God and admitted to myself that I missed the great Creator. I began to chat with God, gradually sharing layers of myself with Him, telling more and more of my story. I awakened bit by bit, as if from a long nap, slowly rebuilding trust in the God that did love me.

In fits and starts, I could feel my soul begin to heal. This gradual healing was reflected in my music, and my "song" blossomed, taking on deeper and truer tones of praise. Old song lyrics took on new meaning as I poured out my love to the Savior, and new songs were born in my spirit, as I began to write love songs to Jesus.

The amazing day came when I finally, and with deep certainty, understood that nothing that had happened to me in my life, either against my will or by my own choices, would ever put me outside of the circle of God's love for me and that I had never been bad or unlovable in the eyes of God. I accepted that, even though I could not see God during the times the perpetrator had violated me, God had always been with me. I came to see that it had been the singing of those Sunday School hymns in my mind that had protected me, allowing me to escape to someplace safe, deep inside myself, where I could be shielded from the worst of the horror that was happening. If this had not been the case, I would not have been able to function and, in all probability, there would have come a time when I would have ended my own life, to free myself of the pain of my existence.

"Can we find a friend so faithful, who will all our sorrows share?"

The perpetrator had stolen so much from me. Even Jesus had been lost to me for a time. I decided that I was not going to let him have my Jesus anymore! Maybe that decision was my epiphany moment.

"All night, all day, angels, keep watching over me!"

These days, my relationship with God, Jesus and Spirit are what I lovingly describe as "fluid". I do not have the blind, simple truth of my childhood, believing in a God who is a bit like a magic Genie in a bottle, who if I wish hard enough, will give me everything I want. But neither am I the person I once was, always secretly angry and disappointed in a God who I believed remained cold, distant and disinterested in my life, while blessing so many others instead. I am somewhere in between.

I know that Jesus always has, and always will, love and care about me. I believe that I am created in the image of the Divine One and am treasured in the eyes of God. I know that on days when I feel hopeless, I can turn to the One who loves me and find my spirit restored, renewed and ready to face another day. These days, I have a new song to sing!*

Today, I spent quality time with Jesus and wrote Him a love song.

Only You

In my storm,

In pouring rain,

When all seems lost,

I bless,

Jesus.

In my empty spaces,

In my barren places,

When there is no other,

I praise,

Jesus.

I trust You,

I love You,

In my heart,

Jesus.

Only You,

Still You

I will praise You,

I will claim You,

I trust You,

Your lovely name,

Jesus!

Your promise,

Your love,

You remain,

Your holy name!

Jesus!

I need You.

There is You,

Always You,

Still You,

Jesus!

Heart to Heart with Spirit

Is there a song in your heart that is waiting to be written? You don't have to be a musician to have a song within you, yearning to be set free.

Is there something on your heart that you would like to share with your Higher Power, by whatever name that connects and calls you into the light of love?

_____

_____

_____

_____

_____

_____

_____

_____

_____

_____

_____

_____

_____

_____

_____

_____

_____

_____

_____

_____

A RESTORATION OPPORTUNITY MOMENT
WITH THE DIVINE

As you are willing and able, allow yourself to rest gently and quietly in the presence of the Divine One and open yourself to the Creator's love for you. Allow yourself to remain still and quiet for a few moments as your body, mind and spirit, settle into stillness as you prepare to engage in the following practice.

Rest… in the Creator's loving arms, holding you gently and carefully, like the treasure you are.

Breathe…in the soft ombre blues of peace, deep into your being.

Receive…the gentle winds of the universe, clearing away all that is unnecessary from your spirit in this moment.

Breathe…deep and allow your mind to become free from the clutter of unwanted thoughts.

Release…the aches and pains held in your body, resulting from the pain in your heart.

Breathe…in the fresh warmth of a spring day.

Restore… all within you that feels parched, cracked and dull. Allow yourself to be soothed with Spirit's restorative balm, smoothing and healing where needed, again and again.

Breathe…in the true knowledge that hope and joy abide within your depths, ready to spring up and flow out, into the bright light of day.

Accept the knowledge that you are Divinely loved, always.

Breathe…in Spirit's call to life.

_____

_____

_____

_____

_____

_____

_____

_____

_____

_____

_____

_____

_____

_____

_____

_____

_____

_____

EIGHT

M IS FOR MOTHER

I have been so very angry with my mother for what feels like most of my life, and I am often exhausted by the weight and depth of my complex feelings for her, feelings that in large part, have been driven by my anger. Sometimes, my anger has pushed me to a place of having to admit that there have been moments when I have hated her in a way that has been hard for me to separate from my love for her. Some days, I have hated myself for loving her.

For years, I thought that I was angry with my mother for failing to love and nurture me as I needed and wanted her to. I was heartsick and disappointed that her love in no way resembled anything close to the love of the mothers I saw on television. Mothers with kind, gentle, and firm, yet supportive and encouraging displays of affection towards their children. Mothers that were tolerant and patient of their children's wrong-doings, large and small, and glowing with pride at their every accomplishment.

I did not understand until much later that these TV moms were created by predominantly white men, with their narrow views of a woman's "place". And that their definition of a socially acceptable, strived for, white middle-class standard of motherly perfection, was nothing more than a fantasy sold to the masses. This fantasy was something that my African American mother would never be capable of achieving, regardless of her social status within her community. The definition of family I saw presented on the TV shows that I so faithfully watched were not rooted in any reality that I knew. Yet sadly, not knowing any better at the time, I judged my mother by these white make-believe moms and found her lacking in many ways.

My relationship with my mother throughout my childhood and adolescence was not an easy one, and most of the time, it felt as though neither of us understood or was ever completely happy with the other. There were no open and honest conversations between us, nor were there any shows of affection freely exchanged with any regularity. But given the secrets that our house was hiding and holding, how could the situation have been any different? Somewhere along the way, part of me gave up hope that my mother would magically morph into some shadings of any one of the TV moms I so cherished.

As I moved into adulthood, my feelings about my mother became even more troublesome to my spirit, keeping my emotions in a swirling cauldron of confusing turmoil. There were days when the mere sound of her voice on the telephone could and did prompt such anger and frustration within me, that my chest would begin to pound and tighten, and feelings of rage would arise within me. This time, it did not take a therapist to help me see that I was harboring a ton of unresolved anger and resentment, topped off with more than a bit of sadness and frustration, towards my mother. These unresolved and supercharged feelings were literally killing me from the inside out, robbing me of the ability to feel and sustain any significant measure of joy and peace in my life.

Maintaining any type of emotionally healthy relationship with my mother seemed almost out of the realm of possibility. I began to understand that if indeed I were to survive and sustain any type of relationship with my mother, aspects of our relationship dynamic had to change, sooner rather than later.

I knew for certain that I could not change anything about my mother and how she communicated with me, but I could begin to change how I responded to and dealt with her. I could begin to better adjust, and possibly change, some of my thoughts about her that repeatedly threatened my happiness and peace of mind. I was not totally sure where to begin in my efforts to create a plan of change designed to help me salvage my sanity, if I were to remain in relationship with my mother. However, I knew that I was going to have to create a plan that involved some combination of healthy mental and emotional "tools" such as therapy, prayer and meditation, that would allow me to manage how I dealt with her.

Right about now, you may be wondering why I didn't just sever all ties with her and live my life without her. Believe me, this has been a question I have repeatedly asked myself over the years, only to arrive at the same conclusion: I still believed that having her in my life, even on limited terms, was a better option for me than moving forward as though I had no mother at all.

One day, after a particularly heart-challenging therapy session and a ton of prayerful discernment around my "mother feelings", I found an answer to part of what my "mother management plan" should include. I was led by Spirit to do something that to me, at the time, felt almost unimaginable: I chose to forgive my mother. Forgive her?! Did I "hear" Spirit correctly? Surely this was not what was being asked of me? Maybe totally walking away from my mother was the better option indeed, because it was an almost unfathomable notion that I could ever forgive her for what was a long, and I felt justified, list of her transgressions towards me. The very idea made both my head and heart hurt.

When I shared my spiritual directive with my therapist, she agreed that this could indeed be an excellent path to pursue. She then proceeded to suggest that we "explore" possible options of how to accomplish what felt, for me, like a daunting task. I, however, was stuck on the word "forgive." How, I wondered, could I possibly forgive the woman who had stood by and done nothing to help me during my years of abuse at the hands of my perpetrator? How could she not have known what was going on right under her own roof? And here I was considering forgiving her! Had I gone mad?!

I wanted every one of my hard-earned therapy dollars back! Or better yet, I would get a new therapist! Yes, at that point, getting a new therapist definitely sounded like a better plan of action than this forgiveness plan.

Kicking and screaming all the way (picture me having a two-year old's tantrum), I began to think about what it would mean for me to forgive my mother. I reviewed my list of all the ways I believed that she had hurt, failed and/or disappointed me. Over time, as I worked on my list and reviewed the things that I had written about my mother's shortcomings, something inside of me began to shift away from my heavy feelings of anger, bitterness, disappointment and concerns about whether it would ever be possible to forgive her. I began to believe in a new truth: I did not need to engage or seek my mother's active participation in order to forgive her. In my prayer time, Spirit confirmed this truth. I could forgive my mother and not engage her. Suddenly, forgiveness felt doable!

Opening myself to the prospect that I did not need to literally "partner" with my mother in my plan to forgive her, allowed me to breathe a bit easier internally. I began to consider how I might facilitate forgiveness towards her in my spirit, without her knowledge or consent. An option rose in my spirit that made sense and felt "right" to me. I could take the entire concept of forgiving my mother off the table for now and instead try extending mercy and compassion towards her in my mind, heart, and prayers. Best of all, I still did not have to deal with her face to face.

In the days ahead, as I continued to pray and meditate on the act of extending mercy and compassion towards my mother, some of the anger that I had carried for so long began to slowly dissipate, creating space in my heart for what would one day become forgiveness. Over time, I began to forgive my mother for not being like the TV fantasy moms I so desperately and naively wished she had been, as well as not being who and what I needed her to be for me, on any given day. Instead, I began to forgive her for being human and flawed; for being imperfect, but still my mother.

In thinking about my mother and some of her more provoking (for me) traits and behaviors, I suspect that she met and struggled with her own unique challenges throughout her life. Challenges that combined brokenness, unhappiness, fears, loss (and more), and that may have put her on her own path of unhealthy decisions and heartache. I do not know her life's story, as my mother is not one to talk about her feelings or personal history. Perhaps one day she will share it with me, although I do not hold out much hope of that happening.

I continue my daily quest of forgiving my mother for being who she is, rather than who she is not. My mother is a multi-faceted individual, possessing many fine, yet taxing qualities that are not always good for me to have too much emotional exposure to. She is not a "bad" or "mean" person, and indeed most people would say that she is sweet, kind, and loving. These same people would, in all likelihood, go on to say just how much they adore her. I'm sure that one or two would nominate her for sainthood, if it was within their power to do so.

I believe that she has loved me within the constraints of her ability to do so at any given time. I have also seen evidence in recent years of the ways in which she seems to be genuinely trying to show her love and care for me, almost as though making amends for past slights and hurts.

There is much more that I could say about my ongoing trials while attempting to maintain a "reasonably" healthy relationship with my mother, but I will save that sharing for another time. In this moment, I will simply say that being regularly exposed to my mother requires a great deal of prayer and creative planning on my part, if I am to remain whole. It also requires that I love myself daily and this allows me to love her, on my terms and in my way.

Extending compassionate, merciful love towards my mother is still not, by any means, an easy task for me to accomplish. In the beginning of this chapter, I dared proclaim that there have been some days when I have hated my mother. For a long time, I had believed this feeling to be true. What I now know to be true, is the fact that I do not hate my mother, but I do despise and reject many of the negative feelings and emotions that her behaviors can activate within me.

However, I strive to choose love over hate, love over resentment, love over anger. This choice requires me to set and keep strong and healthy emotional and mental boundaries in place regarding my mother, and to monitor, and in some cases limit my interactions with her. Some days, I get it all just right, and some days, not so much. Thank God for Jesus and therapy!

My thoughts and experiences related to the subject of mothers and daughters and the twists and turns of how they love, will require its own separate book. Until I decide to write that book, I shall continue my practice of forgiveness extended to my mother. Forgiving her reminds me that we are all in need of mercy, grace and someone else's forgiveness, including me.

A Heart Space Moment

Would now be a good time for you to pause and write some of what's on your heart about your mother, or perhaps a mother figure?

_____

_____

_____

_____

_____

_____

_____

_____

_____

_____

_____

_____

_____

_____

_____

_____

_____

_____

_____

_____

_____

My Truths, Observations and Lessons Learned on Forgiveness, Imprinted on My Heart

(In no particular order, yet of equal importance.)

Forgiveness, like love, is a daily choice, sometimes made moment by moment.

Forgiveness looks and feels different for each person.

Each of us must prayerfully define forgiveness for ourselves, creating our own formula to bring about its happening and opportunity for healing.

At times, we must forgive ourselves before we can begin the process of forgiving others.

Forgiveness happens in its own time and in its own way.

We must be ready to answer the call of forgiveness when it beckons and as our heart allows.

If I am to survive, grow and flourish, daily becoming more of who I believe Spirit is "calling" me to be, I must, with careful intention, create space in my heart for forgiveness to take root. Then, as though tending a beautiful garden, I must be vigilant in ridding my heart of the weeds of unhealthy thoughts and emotions that do not serve me well and could potentially cause destruction to new growth.

Forgiveness happens in "fits and starts" over time, meaning that I have often had to forgive the same person repeatedly, over a lifetime, sometimes for the same transgression.

The path to forgiveness is not always a clear or direct line from point A to point B, but rather more of a circle. Sometimes it forces me (perhaps even you) to travel the same road, again and again, as though wandering aimlessly lost in the woods for a time, only to end where we began and never finding the way home. But if we stay on the path and patiently persevere, forgiveness can and will lead us home, back to the center of our hearts, where we can find peace, and wholeness, if that is what we sincerely desire.

Often, forgiveness is not for the one who has done us harm, but rather for us. This means that forgiveness can take place privately within our spirit, without any direct contact with the person we are forgiving, or without them even being aware that they have done anything that requires our forgiveness.

Forgiveness can act as a release, allowing us to sever unhealthy connections to those who are not good for us. We can forgive and move on.

Discernment is one of the most important elements of forgiveness.

Forgiveness of self and others can help open the heart's door to love.

Being called to forgive does not necessarily mean being called to forget. Sometimes, remembering the source of the hurt or transgression can help us to not further engage the transgressor or repeat the act. Meaning, once you see the hole in the sidewalk and have fallen in, it makes sense to learn a new path to your needed destination.

I choose to forgive myself. Some days, this is hard.

I pray for the sincere humility to seek the forgiveness of others.

Some days, I am better at forgiving than I am on other days.

I will continue my practice of forgiveness, daily, repeatedly.

When you are ready, and as you choose, write your
thoughts and reflections about forgiveness, or anything
else that is on your heart in this moment.

_____

_____

_____

_____

_____

_____

_____

_____

_____

_____

_____

_____

_____

_____

_____

_____

_____

_____

_____

_____

_____

A BREATHING AND SOUL REFRESHING OPPORTUNITY

Perhaps now is a good time for you to stop and breathe in healing and cleansing thoughts, reminding yourself that you are always held safely and deeply within the loving and forgiving gaze of the Divine Creator.

Breathe deeply of Spirit's fresh winds of peace, love, strength, joy and whatever your need in this moment.

With each breath, allow yourself to feel new space being created within your being, so that the longing of your heart can be filled.

Just breathe…

NINE

LAY ASIDE EVERY WEIGHT

"Therefore, since we are surrounded by so great a cloud of witnesses, let us also lay aside every weight" Hebrews 12: 1a NIV

For a significant portion of my life, I have believed that it was my body weight that I had been struggling to "lay aside" or lose. I have always thought that if I could lose (and permanently keep off) the extra pounds, I would somehow be free of the boulders in my soul that held me down and blocked me from experiencing a joyful, light and unencumbered existence. That I could finally feel and be "beautiful".

Over time, God revealed to me that the true source of my weight issues was not rooted in the extra pounds I carried on my body, but rather in the bulk and girth of my own thoughts and the secrets I kept hidden in the folds of my soul. In my past, I have not only been weighed down by the heft of my secrets but, in many ways, I had become comfortable with keeping them. This is a difficult truth to admit about myself. It was not until I became aware of this truth that I understood how I sometimes used my ease with hiding things and maintaining silence to avoid certain truths about myself and others, resulting in harm to my psyche.

Gradually, through my prayer and meditation, God revealed to me that it was time (way past time, if I'm being honest) for me to release and "lay aside" many of the closeted emotional weights that I had carried for so long. It was as though God spoke to the center of my being and lovingly whispered, "I know how tired you are of carrying these burdensome pains on your heart and in your spirit. The issues you have kept deep within are now writing and revealing themselves on your body. This is not what I want for you, my beloved, beautiful daughter. I do not want you to carry these secret weights in your body, mind or spirit. I have created you in beauty and I call you my own."

As God's words poured into my heart, I felt the deep and abiding truth of them begin to steep into my spirit, washing away my long-held hurts and replacing them with God's soothing balm of love. I could feel many of the things that I had so desperately kept buried in the furthest corner of my heart for so long, being gently excavated by the light of God's truth and love for me.

God continued speaking to my heart and began revealing that there was another step required in my process of laying aside my weight and letting go of things that did not serve me well. Not only did God reveal that I was to let go of the various emotional weights that I had carried for so long, God wanted me to refrain from picking them up again.

I tried to play dumb and act as though I was not "tuning in" to that portion of what God was saying to me, but God continued to repeat that part of the message, loud and clear. Finally, I had no choice but to listen and admit that I had indeed released myself from the bondage of various weights in my life, only to turn around and pick them back up again. Instances of me picking up weights that I have previously released occur as a result of my worrying and in some cases obsessing over them. Sometimes it felt almost as though I did not know how to live or who to "be" without these emotional weights in my life. I am ashamed to say that at times, laying aside certain weights felt like neglecting an old friend. Here are three ways this phenomenon has shown up in my experiences:

One: When my perpetrator died, I thought that I was finally free of him and the emotional hold that his presence in my life had held over me.

In fact, it was just the opposite. I found that while I may have been free of the sight of him, I was not totally liberated from the space he occupied in my mind.

The death of my perpetrator started me on a spiral of judging myself harshly for not having done more to expose him for the monster that he was, while he was alive. Rather than affirm and celebrate myself for having survived his demonic wrongs, the pain he caused, and the strides that I had made to heal and create a loving and nurturing life for myself, I found fault within myself, and once again began to look at myself as less than. In other words, I picked back up my "weight" of self-condemnation and shame that I had fought so valiantly and tirelessly to lay aside. I did not treat myself kindly or with care. I did not remember that the shame was his to own and not mine, never mine!

God called me to lay aside the unnecessary and undeserved weight of self-condemnation and emotional self-flagellation. God continuously calls me to remember, know and claim "who I am and whose I am", beautifully created in the image and wisdom of the Divine.

Two: At times, I have allowed people to occupy space in my head and my heart who were not good for me, nor the well-being of my spirit. Even though once I finally saw the person or persons for who they were and let them go, I sometimes allowed them to come back into my heart, all the while knowing that they had the power to hurt me. I allowed this because it was what they wanted and needed, meaning I put the wants and needs of another in front of my own. I picked back up the weight of not valuing the sanctity of my well-being above the selfish desires of others. I gave up my power of "no"!

God calls me to know my true value and lovingly demands and directs that I not give myself away lightly, without care or concern for the cost to me. God wants me to use both my "no and yes powers" with discernment and discretion. God wants me to not be afraid to let someone go who is not good for me and trust that God will fill the space that person had occupied, with things, designed and destined for my good.

Three: I have not always forgiven myself for the times that, when acting out of my brokenness and pain, I have caused heartache to myself and others. I have too often reclothed myself in the weight of unforgiveness, resulting in the needless pains of resentment and hard-heartedness, toward myself and others as well.

God calls me, with infinite grace, to claim the joy of forgiveness and the freedom that it offers my heart, mind and soul. I am further called to extend to myself the gift of gazing upon myself through merciful eyes, thereby creating the opportunity for a more honest definition of love for myself and others.

An Invitation to Dance

Writing this book has helped free me from a great deal of what has pressed down heavily on my heart for so many years. I am more grateful than I can articulate for heeding Spirit's call and direction throughout this process. The completion of this project has helped me to lay aside weight, carried far too long.

As you are able and with gentle care, imagine yourself free and light in spirit dancing unencumbered by any past weights, heartaches or pains. If it is helpful and comfortable for you to do so, try closing your eyes and putting on music. You may even want to experiment with various styles / genres of music to see which selection(s) invite your soul to dance.

Do not be afraid to move to the secret rhythms of your soul's footsteps. Be your own, most excellent choreographer.

_____

_____

_____

_____

_____

_____

_____

_____

_____

_____

_____

_____

_____

_____

_____

I DANCE IN THE LIGHT
OF EACH NEW DAWN

Look deeper, I remind myself,

In the mirror of my soul,

There is beauty there,

Alive, inside, waiting to be revealed,

I dare say, "hello!"

I dance with wanton abandon, naked in my beauty,

Cloaked solely in the shimmering light of Spirit's embrace,

It is enough and I dance on,

I am unafraid of the steps, knowing not the way ahead,

My soul knows and will lead!

TEN

PROMISES TO KEEP

Let us run with endurance the race that is set before us."
Hebrews 12: 1b, NIV

It is my hope that, in your journey through these pages, you have discovered something wonderful and surprisingly delightful about yourself that adds to the joy and fullness of your days.

If you have gleaned insights about your life's story that have not settled well or lightly within you, be gentle and forgiving as you examine them, or not, as your heart allows. Please do not judge yourself harshly.

I pray that you embrace the knowledge that you are indeed stronger than you think and that you can "go the distance and run your race" with grace, purpose, love, and peace, while opening yourself to Spirit's plan for your good.

Writing this book has afforded me the opportunity for meaningful exploration of my heart's truths, needs and desires. My process of writing this book has also challenged me to remember that there are promises I must make and keep for myself, for the good of all that I am and all that I aspire to be. I am content to be a seeker of my own spirit's truth.

I share with you now the promises that I am making and plan to keep for my mental, emotional, and spiritual well-being moving forward.

My Promises to Keep

I will cherish myself as the treasure God has created me to be.

I will seek peace and joy.

I will value my own innate wisdom.

I will not harm myself with direct intent in any way.

I will remove myself from the presence of unhealthy and potentially harmful energy of others who do not value me.

I will practice forgiveness of myself and others daily, or as needed.

I will stand naked in front of the largest mirror in my home and tell myself that I am beautiful.

I will dance naked in my soul's mirror, daring to claim my destiny.

I will not allow my beauty to be defined by others.

I will continue my journey of healing.

I will deepen my connection to God and seek Spirit's voice and direction.

I will let love lead.

I will pray for peace in the world.

I will make choices that allow me to be an instrument of peace and justice.

I will allow myself to see past the scars of my past and open my eyes to my bright future.

I will embrace the knowledge that a new and melodious song is being written on my soul every day and I will sing it!

In moments of distress, I must remind myself of these truths:

I am strong!

I am worthy!

I deserve good things!

I am so much more than the things that were done to me!

I choose me! I can and will write my own story!

One Last Opportunity for Your Reflection and Introspection Before We Part, Brave Reader

As you reflect on the word "promise", open your entire being to the loving task of answering the following questions. Always remember, there are no right or wrong answers. There is only the truth of discerning and welcoming your heart's desire and soul's yearning for the bliss of harmony within.

What does the word "promise" mean to you, as you continue your work of self-discovery, healing and empowerment?

_____

_____

_____

_____

_____

_____

_____

_____

_____

_____

_____

_____

_____

_____

_____

_____

_____

What are the promises and assurances that your heart needs to hear from you? List them without care or thought to prioritizing. Let your heart lead the way.

_____

_____

_____

_____

_____

_____

_____

_____

_____

_____

_____

_____

_____

_____

_____

_____

_____

_____

_____

_____

_____

_____

What vows can you make to your heart in this moment, to help ensure that you honor your soul's pledge to your continued well-being?

A FINAL WORD

I began in Chapter One by addressing you, Brave Reader, and inviting you into portions of my life's journey. We have traveled far and, at times, the way may not have always felt calm or easy. However, we persevered and here we are, at the end. Just as I said "hello", I bid you now "adieu".

Thank you for opening yourself to this journey of discovery and introspection with me.

I hope and pray that you have learned at least one glorious truth about your own strength and worth that will assist you as you travel forward, attending lovingly and patiently to your process of continued healing.

Blessed be…

RESOURCES

SONGS MENTIONED IN CHAPTER SEVEN

Jesus Loves Me
text, A. B. Warner, tune CHINA, refrain, W. B. Bradbury

Love Lifted Me
text, J. Rowe, tune, SAFETY

Jesus Loves the Little Children
text. C. H. Woolston, tune, CHILDREN, G. F. Root

Blessed Assurance
text, F. Crosby, tune, ASSURANCE, P. Knapp

I Must Tell Jesus
text, E. A. Hoffman, tune, ORWIGSBURG

I Need Thee Every Hour
text A. S. Hawkes, tune, NEED, R. Lowry

Amazing Grace
text, J. Newton, tune, NEWBRITAIN

O How I Love Jesus
text, F. Whitfield, tune, HOW I LOVE JESUS

What a Friend We Have in Jesus
text, J. M. Scriven, tune, A. Lowery

All Night, All Day
Spiritual

PROFESSIONAL CONSULTANTS

Dr. Deborah G. Haskins, Licensed Clinical Professional Counselor,
Owner/Chief Clinical Consultant MOSAIC Consulting and
Counseling Services
Hello@drdeborahhaskins.com
www.drdeborahhaskins.com

Àjíké Kendrick Aşegún, MA
Organizational & Executive Life Coach
Spiritry: Leadership Development through Spirituality
www.spiritry.com
info@spiritry.com

Dr. Satira Streeter, Licensed Clinical Psychologist
Ascensions Psychological and Community Services, Inc.
www.2ascend.org

NATIONAL RESOURCES

Darkness to Light
866-For-Light (367-5444)

RAINN
National Sexual Assault Telephone Hotline
800-656-HOPE (4673)
www.rainn.org

Survivors of Incest Anonymous

Siawso.org

877-742-9761

National Suicide Prevention Hot line

800-273-8255

Suicidepreventionlifeline.org